THOUGHT CATALOG BOOKS

The Single Girl's Guide To Living And Laughing (And Sometimes Loving)

The Single Girl's Guide To Living And Laughing (And Sometimes Loving)

ALEXANDRIA BROWN

THOUGHT CATALOG BOOKS

Brooklyn, NY

THOUGHT CATALOG BOOKS

Copyright © 2016 by Alexandria Brown

All rights reserved. Published by Thought Catalog Books, a division of The Thought & Expression Co., Williamsburg, Brooklyn. Founded in 2010, Thought Catalog is a website and imprint dedicated to your ideas and stories. We publish fiction and non-fiction from emerging and established writers across all genres. For general information and submissions: manuscripts@thoughtcatalog.com.

First edition, 2016

ISBN 978-1945796180

10 9 8 7 6 5 4 3 2 1

Cover design by © KJ Parish

Dedicated to so many friends and family that this would be seven pages long by the time I finished. Just know that I appreciate everyone who's been a part of this journey.

To my person. Thanks for always being the strength in my weakest moments and for never letting me down. For those two things alone I owe you more than you'll ever know. All my love always.

Also for Kendra Syrdal. For writing the foreword. For always listening to my babble and reading my stuff. For every single fantastic piece of wisdom. I wouldn't be anywhere close to here without you. Check her out on Twitter (@kendrasyrdal). Seriously... do it.

And finally for you. Your presence amongst these pages have not gone unnoticed to me. And wherever you are I hope you're happy, healthy and loved. That's all I've ever wanted for you.

Contents

Part IV. The Heartbreak

Part V. The Love

Foreword

Kendra Syrdal

On December 21st, 2015, I was two weeks into a new job, terrified that I was underqualified and constantly questioning whether or not I could actually spot quality writing, when I came across an essay by a girl named Alexandria Brown. It was a simple little essay about never wanting the butterflies of falling for someone to go away. But simple as it was, something about it struck me. There was a toughness that was still soft, a vulnerability that was still careful and methodical. It was the kind of writing that didn't come out and slap you across the face with its message, but still left a mark none-the-less.

There was something about it, no matter how unobvious or unassuming, that made me smile.

So I hit publish. And that was my introduction to Alex and her incredibly honest and purposeful way of looking at butterflies, being single, and (of course) love.

See, what I've come to realize as I've gotten to know Alex more and read her writing is that the mark of good writing, of writing that truly matters, is just that it does something to you. While I was sitting there, questioning whether or not I could spot quality writing in an inbox with unread essays totaling near 1500, I really only needed to remember one thing:

Good writing, quite simply, makes you feel something.

Even if that something is soft. Even if that something is quiet.

Even if that something is the simple memory of what it feels like to have butterflies in your stomach once again.

And I can, without question, guarantee that Alex's writing will do that and more.

Single girls out there have had butterflies, have fallen in love, have had great sex and not-so-great sex, have questioned their sanity after an orgasm, have loved so deeply and intensely it's scared them, have had their heart ripped out of their chests, have been absolutely sure they'll never feel so strongly about another person ever again, and at the end of it all, have just wondered, "What the hell am I even feeling?"

And Alex is no exception. The only difference is that she's written about exactly what it's like to feel all of the above and more.

This book is a lot of things. It's deep and unapologetic at times, more quiet and simplistic in others. It will make you laugh, it will make you cry, it will make you question and remember everything you've ever learned about love. It will make you feel all of the different emotions, complex and beautiful, about what it truly means to be a single girl who is just looking for love.

But most of all, it's sure to give you butterflies.

—Kendra Syrdal, Producer at Thought Catalog

Part 1

The Single

1

This Is Why You Need To Stop Worrying About Being Single In Your 20s

Let's take five minutes and look at the positives. That person who let you go did you a favor. I know it sounds like a crazy thought but it's true. Right now, you feel like you're never going to love again because you know what love feels like and that was it. Love only comes once in your life. Love only comes to those who deserve it.

Bullshit. Total and utter bullshit.

We get hurt in this life multiple times by multiple people. Sometimes by friends, lovers, or even family. But life doesn't just stop because of this. Does it momentarily feel like the world is caving in? Yes. It totally does. I know because I've been there, too. But I'm never going to give up on love even though right now I can tell you it feels like I'm never going to do it again. Four years later, actually, and I'm still trying to figure out if it'll show up on my doorstep again.

But while love is taking its time to get to you, think about the amazing things you can do as a single person right now. You don't owe anybody anything. Do you want to stay out all night and not have to check in? Do you want to sleep with the hot stranger across the bar? Do you want to travel the world and not have to cater to someone else's travel itinerary? Right now is the time to do it.

You will never be as a free as you are right now.

Some day soon you're going to have so many responsibilities you won't know what to do with them. You'll feel overwhelmed and wish for the day when the only person you had to worry about making a decision for was you.

Yes sometimes it gets lonely. Sometimes I want to feel the sparks and excitement that come from being in love but I also know that I'm not capable of that. It's OK to be completely selfish and find yourself. It's OK to want to freely date multiple people at the same time. It's OK to pack a weekender and just leave for as long as you want.

I used to think 25 was the year I was going to get my shit together. I was going to settle down and maybe have a long-term relationship with someone stable. Someone who has their shit together, as well. But life doesn't work that way. Age doesn't define when you should or shouldn't do things. Age also doesn't define maturity. Get married and have a family when you want to.

It's always going to be your choice.

When you start feeling a victim of your circumstances is when you've failed yourself. You are not weak. You are not wrong.

You are where you are supposed to be right now. And if you're not happy with something? Change it.

Whether you're single or not, you do not need to settle for anything. You are smart. You are courageous. You can do whatever you set your mind to. You have one life to live so why waste it feeling like you're only half alive?

Love will find you when it's supposed to, if it hasn't already.

Our society makes it seem like the only thing in life to live for is another person. That's not true. Some of us are meant to find the love of our lives and be completely, stupidly happy with them till the end of our days. But some of us are meant for something else.

Humans are inherently different with separate paths. If you stay true to yours and follow it, then you are completely doing what you should be. Everything else will fall into place.

2

These Are The Things You Learn When You're A Total Hopeless Romantic

Is there ever a point in our lives where we should give up on love? Where we should throw in the towel and just be content with not finding another person to let into our hearts? I don't think so. I don't think that we should ever look at life and think that love will never find us.

But this is all coming from a hopeless romantic. Mostly hopeless. And being a hopeless romantic in the modern age has taught me a lot of lessons all about love.

1. Prince Charming might ride the bus instead of a white horse.

Does what we drive or what we wear or what we do really matter at the end of the day? Why do we set impossible high standards on what we're looking for in another person so that it makes it so that when we do find someone, they have to meet a criteria list that literally not many people can? When you find someone who makes you happy, the details really are just the details.

2. Sometimes the person you love doesn't magically realize they love you, too.

Sometimes we fall for people who don't feel the same way. Does that mean that in some way we've failed either physically or personality wise? No. Not at all. I have found that sometimes falling for the wrong person can teach us what we want from the right person.

3. You have to kiss a lot of frogs.

Or maybe you didn't have to and are just lucky. Sometimes, though, it takes a long time till you find the one person you want to settle down and have a house full of puppies with. Just because it's taking a long time to find the one though doesn't mean that there's anything wrong with you. It just means that they're taking their sweet-ass time to get to you.

4. Nothing good comes without struggle.

Even when you meet the right person, that doesn't mean you ride off into the sunset and that's it. You just get to live your life with your love without any sort of issues. Nope. No way. Whoever said love isn't work is extremely stupid. Love is another full-time job on top of your already full-time job.

Even though it takes work, it's the most fulfilling job in the world if you find the right partner to do it with.

5. Sparks fade, but laughs don't.

You know that fuzzy feeling in your tummy you get when that new person you're into texts you? Yeah, that fades. It just has to. It deepens into something more than just butterflies. So if you're the type of person who lives for sparks, I'm sorry to tell you that it's not real. Find someone you can be incredibly silly with. Find the person who you stay up all night with laughing with. That's the person you should want to end up with. Not the one with instant sparks.

6. Never settle.

My last and probably the most important point: never settle. For anything or anyone. Resentment isn't something you want to feel later on in life. You want to look at the person you've ended up with and see what you saw in them the first time you met. Fall in love with the person for everything that they are and everything they add to your life. Never let someone make you feel like you can't do better because if that person is not making you feel your absolute best. I promise you can find better.

Your happily ever after might not have a sunset or royalty but it will match whatever reality you've created. From one hope-less romantic to another, falling in love isn't always sunshine and rainbows, but it is worth diving into. No matter what happens at the end of the day, love will always be the best feeling.

3

Read This If You Feel Like You'll Never Be The Girl They Date

I was 18 the first time a guy told me I wasn't the girl you date. I had no idea what he meant because I had assumed for the last two months that we were, in fact, dating. I had waited two months to even sleep with him. After we hooked up, I asked him where this was going he causally rolled over to me and said, "You're not the girl I'm dating, you're just the girl I'm fucking." I was confused because that was literally the first time we had even had sex. But then again, I was only 18.

Over the next few years, I would hear different versions of the same lines from men.

Well I really like you as a friend.
I would definitely marry you but I'm not ready to settle down.
I just don't think of you like that.

After the third time I started to roll my eyes. I started to be able to numb myself from hearing this. Sometimes I'd just cut them off completely and tell them not to worry about it. Then I did the thing I shouldn't have done: I started to embrace it.

I was on a pretty self-destructive path and it took my best

friend telling me how hard it was to watch me do this time and time again that really made realize that I was part of the problem. Hell, I *was* the problem.

Yeah, men treated me like I wasn't the girl they would marry but I had also let them.

I let them because in some sick way it gave me power which fulfilled the role of love for a long time in my life.

My best friend was tired of hearing about the current married man sending me inappropriate text messages or the douchebag who only texted me late at night. I've even pushed aside nice guys because I knew they weren't going to be able survive my self-proclaimed persona.

She was tired and so was I, but it didn't actually change anything. I wasn't ready to hear what she was really saying. She was basically telling me to value myself more. Maybe that's why now my mission in life is to make sure that all people have some form of self-love. Self-love will save you from this path that I have taken myself down too many times to count. Maybe it's just the simple fact that broken people attract other broken people.

I read somewhere that when two people have sex their souls intertwine and that means that when, for whatever reason, you end a sexual relationship with someone, they will always have a small piece of your soul. I laughed the first time I read that but now it's something I believe in. Giving yourself to someone isn't something you should just do on a whim, it's something you should do when you care a lot for a person. I'm not preaching abstinence but I am preaching that you have no doubts that this person is someone who deserves you.

What really made me decide to no longer embrace this fun and often harsh fact was a conversation with my mom. We have a pretty unconventional relationship that features very few filters on my end, so I would say she knows basically everything that's happened to me in my life. My phone was exploding with text messages and she point-blank said to me it must wear on me that men I was "seeing" often only thought of me late at night. I think my mouth dropped. It's a thought I had in my head but not one that I let out. Hearing it from your own mother, let me tell you, is the hardest thing you'll ever hear.

So I made a decision to change.

Do I still slip back into old habits? Yes. Do I make a conscious effort to value myself more? Definitely. So to the girl that is told in any form that they're only good for sex: I see you, I hear you, and I feel you. I'm here to tell you that this isn't who you have to be. Do whatever it is that makes you happy, but don't do it because someone else decided that's who you are. I've said it before and I'll say it again; you are enough.

This is one part of very many pieces of me. As soon as you start to admit the damaged parts of yourself, is when you can start to heal. Don't be ashamed of your past. Embrace it. Acknowledge it. Then move on. Life is all about figuring out what works for you. So do that and screw (or don't screw) the rest.

4

Read This If You're Completely Terrified Of Being Vulnerable With Someone

Sometimes I wish I could not be as strong as I am. Sometimes I wish I could just break completely open and let out everything I've held so close to my heart. When someone tells me I'm a strong person, I thank them. Internally, I'm happy my façade is working.

Being strong to me is when you're able to be vulnerable with another human being. It's easy to look at someone and assume that because they're smiling, joking around, and looking genuinely happy that everything is going great for them. Don't get me wrong, most of the time things are going pretty great for me. I have amazing friends and family, a job, and I'm overall pretty comfortable. But comfortable has and always will scare me.

I used to own only enough stuff that I could fit into the back of my Mazda 3. The permanence of my situation had never bothered me because everything in my life up until a few years ago was temporary. I could easily pick everything up and leave without a second thought, and I did that a couple of times. My friends used to call me a gypsy because I *was* a gypsy.

This need for temporary led me to a lot of relationships that were definitely not going to last. Three weeks was my max before I started to need to get out. I panicked and looked at the other person as if they're the enemy. They're going to see deep down to the very dark parts of me and judge it all. I'm a runner. I've always been a runner.

So maybe that's where the attraction to men who can't ever fully be with me comes in. It's easy to date someone who's temporary and can't even be permanent even if you wanted them to.

If you never want to be vulnerable, being with someone who's distracted by their own shit is the perfect way to get out of your own. I never had to be fully honest because it's not like it matters. They were only around temporarily.

When you fall in love, you share those scary parts with your other half. When you find your person, you won't feel as though they're going to judge you for your insecurities or vulnerabilities. They're going to be there when you fall apart with their arms open wide so you can place your head on their chest and hear their heartbeat. Their heartbeat will remind you that we're all human. We all have blood pumping through our veins. We all have insecurities.

It's easy to remember the times you were less than stellar and keep those as proof that your pattern is more just the way it is now. That there's no way you can change and be happy with permanent. I've watched my friends get married, have kids, buy houses, or find their version of stable. These are the factors that make me believe that age is really just a number.

I never realized how hard it would be having to see and examine the worst parts of me. I know I'm not some horrible person who kicks puppies on the weekend, but I do have some skeletons buried deep in my closet that have started to bubble to the surface. As my getaway feeling grows stronger, so does the need to let out all of those deep dark secrets I thought I had buried so well.

I can see the bags under my eyes from the sleepless nights of tossing and turning. I see the bloodshot eyes that come from the irritating memories that make the tears fall late at night when I'm alone with just me. I feel the anxiety in the pit of my stomach when the morning rolls around which means that I have to get out of my bed and face the world as if nothing is wrong.

Ultimately we all have a breaking point. We all have a moment where we need to just get away or face the music. From one runner to another, if you stay still long enough maybe you can face your fears and forgive yourself.

5

Maybe We're Not Ready For Love, And Maybe That's Okay

I know in this day and age, wanting a love out of a storybook is completely hopeless. I know that our world moves too fast for us to slow down and pick a flower for the ones we love. I know it's unrealistic to show up to my office and see the person I've been missing magically sitting at my desk. I know that someone isn't going to come up to me and say, "You're the one I've been waiting for."

I know all of those things, but yet I still think about them like they're a possibility. That one day in the middle of the night I'm going to get a call from someone who just can't stop thinking about me and that'll be the way our new adventure together starts. That someone is going to remember that I love frozen yogurt with M&Ms. That someone's going to know that the way to my heart is a gluten-free burger. They're going to remember all the little details that make me, well, *me* and love them all.

But love in this day and age is tricky. We find ourselves trying to love out of convenience. When it's good for us we stick with it but if it's not good then we find something else. We look for the relationship that doesn't take work instead of the one that could enhance our lives if we just put a little effort into it. I'm not blaming one gender over the other because I've seen both make similar decisions when put to the test.

And no one is wrong on how they approach love. Wanting to be in love and putting yourself out there is gutsy. It takes time to build a relationship that works. It takes effort to get to know someone inside and out. It takes work to meet your love, fall in love, and stay in love. It's a full-time job that if you slack off, could cost you everything.

But some of us aren't ready for that yet.

We're not ready to take the jump. And we have to take a jump because being pushed into something we're not ready for isn't going to end well. And boy do we have the pressure to fall in love thrown in our face by outsiders often. Some people are lucky enough to right now be experiencing the highs and lows of being in a relationship. But others, well, we're just trying to stay afloat and find ourselves.

Falling for someone is the scariest, most exhilarating thing you'll ever experience. And if you find the person that makes you feel alive then you hold onto them. But it's OK to not be ready to do that yet. Sometimes we get hurt so bad that thinking about loving a new person feels crippling.

But we do it. We fall in love again when we're ready. Sometimes when we're not. And it happens when we least expect it. We don't expect to be completely blown away by someone's beauty and intensity but it happens. And when it happens you forget those feelings of uncertainty. We forget how much it hurt at the time when we loved the last person. We forget everything and anything that's not with this person right here right now.

So maybe I'll be waiting for a while.

Maybe I'll be waiting a while for the guy who will know that the way to make me feel better is to just hug me and listen to what's on my mind. Or that sometimes I don't want to talk, I just want to laugh. But I'm going to wait for that because settling just isn't an option.

So when you're single and lonely, remember that there is someone worth waiting for. That even if you don't know them right now, they could be just waiting for you to get to them. And when you see each other, you'll just know that this is what you've been preparing for.

Part 2

The Feelings

6

Everyone Thinks We're Wrong For Each Other, But They Just Don't Understand

They don't know. They don't know that I've waited my entire life to meet you. That I've wondered what you were like. That I've dreamt about who we would be together. They don't know that now that you're here, I'm becoming a person I never knew I could be. They don't know. Or maybe they do.

But if they did know, they wouldn't tell me to stop. To not love you simply because they're afraid I'll get hurt. Or that I'll hurt you. Or that we'll self-destruct together. They don't want us to get so lost in each other that we won't be able to find our way back. And they're just as worried as I am that we're only temporary. That this is only temporary.

They don't know about the conversations we have that make us see a future together. If they did, they'd never question our intentions. They would let us be and let us figure out what we're doing as partners rather than strangers. They would let us grow together, and individually, because this love is something that's made for both of us. Not anyone else.

What I do know is this: we're supposed to be here. We're supposed to be right here, right now doing this. Doing this thing together. And you need the inspiration that I can provide just like I need the relaxation that comes just from being around you. I know that we're meant to tell each other our secrets late at night and encourage each other to follow our dreams. **That while we're both completely lost right now, we're also found because we found this and we're doing this. Together.**

They don't know about the doubt. The doubt that we're both feeling because it feels too right. It does feel too right doesn't it? Like sometimes when it's just the two of us and we're talking about nothing, everything in the universe is aligned.

But they do know about our struggles. They do know how we've managed to fall so fast so quick that we've almost skipped the initial phase of just getting to know each other. We've gotten so deep so fast that they're scared it'll fizzle out. And what if it does? What if we wake up one day and realize that we did everything in fast forward and it's too hard to go back now? Back to when things were just us and just this.

They also know how much I can't figure out how to believe that I'm enough for you. That I'm worried that when I see that distant look in your eye, that you're thinking about what you're missing out on. And it's not anything you've done because you've been nothing but there, but just my own insecurities reminding me how every time before you and every time I felt this before, it was ended in my heart break.

But they don't know you. They don't know how amazing you are in your own right. They don't know that all I can think about is you. That everything that you represent for me is hope. That you came at a time when I needed you the most. That you taught me and are still teaching me patience. You're teaching me that I should always keep the faith. **Faith that no matter what, this is going to work out the way it should.**

That's between you and me. Our secret. Our secret to keep and whisper to each other. What's between you and me is so much better than what everyone else thinks they know. Because it is all speculation on their part. That they know better than us. That they see the end. Even if they're right and this ends with us both in complete and utter pain, we know that we had to do this. We had to give us a chance. Because us was better than you or I alone.

They don't know about our love but we do. And that's enough for us.

7

This Is Falling In Love With The Possibility Of Someone

You let out a breath of air as you look up at your ceiling. Every time you close your eyes, you see their face. And it's not irritating. It's just captivating. So captivating it's keeping you up at night. But why are they even in your brain? It's not like you like them. You promised yourself after the last time that no one was going to break down the extremely high walls you've built around your heart.

But you can't get their stupid face out of your mind. So you're awake. Their face isn't actually even dumb at all. It's beautiful. It's so beautiful that you wonder what it would be like to trace your pointer finger from their forehead down to their perfectly shaped lips. They're also not only physically beautiful; they're that *truly* beautiful that scares you. They're smart. They're passionate. They're funny.

They're everything interesting that makes you wonder how people like them exist.

And they do exist. They're not the figment of your imagination that you've dreamt of. They're real life, breathing humans that make you want to dive in again. That makes you forget that for a split second that your ex ever existed.

Then you let your mind start to drift to what they're doing right now in this very instance; that maybe right now, across town they're awake thinking of you, too. That maybe, *just maybe*, this time you're not just dreaming about your future. **Maybe they are your future.**

Then the negativity sets in. What if they're not sleeping by themselves right now? Just because there's a side in your bed that's empty doesn't mean that the object of your affection is also alone. That's what you're thinking isn't it? You think that the powerful feeling you felt when your hands brushed was only one sided and that you're crazy. You're insane enough to believe that this beautiful person could ever feel the same way about you.

You're alone for a lot of reasons remember? You wanted that empty side of the bed next to you because it was once filled with all of your hopes and dreams but now, now it was just empty disappointment. Because you did love before. You loved so hard and so deep but it wasn't enough. Now here you are, awake, thinking about letting yourself be that vulnerable again. You're thinking about placing your battered and bruised heart into the hands of another person who could just crush you.

Once you weren't afraid of love. You weren't so crippled by the thought of letting someone new take your hand and lead you down a new path of love but you are now. Because every trip you've taken has ended with nothing but heartache, and there was no way you were going to let yourself go there again. No matter how beautiful the next person is.

But they are beautiful. And then your mouth twitches for a second before you let yourself smile thinking about the crinkles by their eyes when their face lights up. You let out a small chuckle when you remember how much you laughed at that internet puppy meme together. Your heart stings a bit when you think about how they talked about their own heartache.

It reminds you that no one is exempt from experiencing heartbreak.

It reminds you that even though they're amazing in every way; what you look like, what you've been through, and who you are doesn't determine your ability to be loved.

Your fingers start to burn. You just want to text them and see if they're still up. If they have that one thing to say to you that will ease your mind and give you hope that your feelings are matched. All you really want to text them is *give me love, please.*

Lying in your room, looking up at your ceiling, you take a deep breath and let it out. In that moment you make yourself a promise. Love will come and go but if it does go, it wasn't because you weren't enough. It was because life has a way of teaching us lessons that we need in order to get where we're going.

Then your mind drifts back to that beautiful person entrancing your mind, keeping you from sleep and you smile. You smile because this person reminds you of possibilities and that life is full of them. That feeling you feel right now is *hope*. And that in itself is a beautiful thing.

8

The Truth About Accepting The Things We Cannot Change

It's a tricky feeling, you know? Trying to figure out when to give the person you love space and when to smother them in all the love you have. Giving someone space is one of those things we think that we learn at a young age, but as we get older we discover that with texting and social media we're not really ever getting the space we need.

And we all need space. Space to deal with what we're going through. Space to know if what we're doing is right. Space to just find ourselves. And when you're with someone, giving them space isn't exactly a decision that's easily made. We often find ourselves trying to hold them as tightly as possible because allowing them to even breathe something different would mean the end for us.

But that isn't true. **Letting someone go and find themselves doesn't mean we're losing them.** It means we're letting them grow into the person they need to become. And maybe your love will change, but more than likely it will be for the better. Because holding someone tightly until they suffocate will more likely make them resent you instead of love you.

All we want to do is hold them closer when they want to explore and leave because we need them. And that's OK. It's OK to feel scared when we feel change because change is fucking scary. **No one looks at change as something that's easy and if they do then they're not actually experiencing change.**

Just like we have to sometimes let our loved ones go, we ourselves have to go explore. To see the world and find out what it has to offer us. What we want and what we don't going forward all leads back to what we discover about ourselves in times that are silent.

Silence, though scary, is our friend. It's the friend that forces us to listen to what our thoughts and inner desires have been trying to tell us. It's the friend that gives the sweet relief you sometimes need so desperately. It's also sometimes the loneliest thing in our life.

But we need it. We need to enjoy the silence and learn from it. We need to listen to what our brains are trying to tell us in those most honest moments. We have to decide whether or not we need to listen more so in order to find ourselves or just to take a minute and breathe. **And we need to let go.**

We need to let ourselves let go of the people we love because they will come back if they're meant to. That trust is the hardest of them all. Holding onto something so tight and hoping they don't go. But if they're meant to then they will. It's the way that it works.

I know how it feels to let someone go that you love deeply and I also know how it feels when they decide to not come back. It's because that was their path and their destiny while mine is completely separate.

It's hard to not get lost inside someone else's world and not completely lose sight of your own. **But you do need a path of your own.** You should walk with yourself and know that person before giving everything to another. You alone are enough and you will enhance someone else's life with your own passion for yours.

So embrace change. Learn from it. Love it. Ultimately you'll grow from it.

9

Read This If You're Convinced You're Never Going To Love Again

I see where you're coming from.

You feel like the consistent factor in a long line of broken hearts and bad relationships. You feel like there's something *wrong* with you. That there's something you're doing that makes the relationship end. Something you're doing specifically is creating every single bad ending.

But let me tell you this: everyone is the constant factor in their relationship endings until they meet the right person.

The right person isn't going to walk away with things get tough; that's for the wrong person to do. They're going to wander away when things get tough. You're going to hate them for things that they do that you wished they wouldn't. You're going to feel like there's something missing. Something you can't quite put your finger on. *Until it's over.* When it's over you're going to breathe a little easier even though it hurts.

Because the wrong person won't be able to fill the role of the right one just because you want them to. And there could be nothing wrong with them. There's definitely nothing wrong with you. You're just two people who tried to make something work that was never going to in the first place. And that, my dear, is no one's fault.

When it comes to a risky investment, you're always advised of the odds, and let me tell you, they always look pretty bleak. **But the right payoff, man, that *payoff*, will make those odds seem incredibly worth it.**

And it's always a risk falling in love. A risk that sometimes takes a while to see if the payoff is coming or not. It's one that keeps you on your toes and has you wondering, is this it? Is this the gamble I've been waiting to take?

There'll be something in the pit of your stomach that tells you that it's right. That is this the one that you've been wanting since you started realizing that love is something you need. We're really good at convincing ourselves to settle. That as long as we're loving someone than that's good enough. But you shouldn't settle. **Never, ever settle.**

Time will stand still when you meet that person. The one that's meant to stick around. You won't just lust for them. You won't just get excited about the fact that you get to be in their space. You won't feel like you need them. You will crave them. You will want them. **You will love them so fully that your definition of love right now isn't even close to what it feels like.**

But you're going to waver. Because this is a long journey that some people find early but others find late. You're going to envy your friends. You're going to have days where you don't even care if it ever comes. You're going to ride this roller-coaster until it comes. Until your eyes connect with the person that makes your soul tingle. The one who will open your heart and make you feel things you didn't know existed.

This isn't easy. It's not a path for the faint of heart. It's one you're going to battle down every day. It's a game that will take all of your strength to win. You're allowed to have bad days. You're allowed to feel like you're unlovable (no matter how untrue that is). And you're allowed to think that this person doesn't exist. That they simply cannot and will not make it to you.

But sweetheart, when you least expect it. When you're not sure if you're ready. When your heart tells you that even if you don't meet that person, you'll be OK. That's when you'll meet them. That's when they'll come into your life.

So hold out for that moment. Always believe in love. But more importantly believe that you, as you are, deserve love.

10

I've Learned That I Loved You And That I Can Live Without You

I really wish I could call you. That's all I want to do. Even though you found another me, a *better* me, I just want to talk to you. I want to hear your voice. I want to know that the feelings we felt weren't as easily replaceable as it seemed. Because you replaced me so seamlessly, so easily, that it almost feels like we weren't ever even together.

So we can compare lives. We can compare where we're at. We can look at everything that I have and everything you have. And if people were looking at who won, it would be you. You have someone who loves you while I have a one-bedroom apartment to myself. You have a family and roots while I have wanderlust and a gypsy lifestyle. You go to bed with the same person every night while I still wake up sometimes with different people.

Our friends forget that if there's one name they shouldn't mention, it's yours. And they tell me things. Things about how you're doing. If you're happy. If the love that you found all those years ago is still as fulfilling as the day you left. And I see pictures from time to time of you with her and your new family and I wonder if you ever think about the girl you left behind.

But I'm no longer that girl.

I've grown up. I've seen things. I've learned the harsh realities of how feelings really can fuck you over. How sometimes being in love with someone doesn't mean that they love you back. That even though you want to control your emotions and move on that love isn't logical. It isn't a puzzle you can just solve and that's it. It's over. And everything is fine.

Because if it was then maybe I'd be just as happy with someone new of my own. I'd have a family. I'd have roots. I wouldn't have the itchy feeling in my feet every time something started to feel more and more permanent. If someone started to feel too permanent. It's not that I don't want those things; it's just that I've felt how much it hurts when you lose them and watch the person you love have it with someone else.

But then I remember everything I've done. Everything I've seen. Everyone I've met.

I remember how happy you were not going anywhere and how much that drove me crazy. I remember that even though I loved you and even though I romanticized our past that my future has been completely and utterly paved by the shattered pieces of the heart that you broke. That heartbreak has led me to do things I wouldn't have done if I was still with you.

It might sound crazy, but I'm happy you're happy. I'm happy that you met someone who gives you everything I couldn't.

Because she *did* give you everything I couldn't. I was never meant to be your forever and neither were you mine. We were in each other's lives temporarily to realize that the feelings we had with each other exist. But that we can find them with other people. That we can love fully and hard without fear of losing.

When I lost you I thought I lost everything. I thought that I was going to be one of those people who stopped trying. I thought that there was no way that my heart was going to heal. And even though it stings a bit when I hear your name. Or maybe I feel nostalgic for the great times. I know that we were meant to be on the separate paths we're on now.

And I love you for everything you've done for me. You taught me what it was like to love and lose.

But mostly you taught me how to feel things I've would have never learned how to without you. I've learned that I loved you and that I can live without you.

Part 3

The Sex

11

For That Rare Person Whose Love Is Like An Addiction

I want you to drag your fingertips from the top of my shoulder past my forearm until you stop at my fingertips. I want to feel the electricity that comes from your touch. Body on body. The ultimate feeling of vulnerability. The best high that we as humans can experience. I want that rush again.

It's an addiction. A longing. A want so deep that it keeps me up at night. When you run your hands through my hair and my eyes close is when I know that I don't want you to stop. It's a moment so pure that it just couldn't be replicated. There's something in your eyes that make me realize that this is more than recreational. It's a deep-seeded need.

I want to be your fix. Something you crave so badly that you can't help but reach for your phone any time of the night to call me. You need the temporary high just like I do.

It's not love, but it's sure as hell a good enough replacement. If it continues it'll be a bad habit that neither of us can kick.

Sometimes you meet someone and the connection so raw, so authentic that you can't deny it. When you stand close to them you feel your fingers start to burn. You just want to run a thumb across their cheek. You want to grab their wrists and pin them against the wall. When they look deep into your eyes you'd swear they're burning a hole in your soul. One that will always scream their name.

This kind of raw attraction is rare. It's so rare I swear it's primal. It's the kind of attraction that makes you desire nothing else. You wonder if it's going to feel that good again. And then it does feel that good again.

It's a wanting. A needing. A feeling that won't just simply go away.

You try to act normal because that's all you can do to keep going with your life but your daydreams always bring you back to that person. You know one more taste is going to be so bittersweet because it's not love and you know that. You know deep down inside that this person isn't the one but they definitely are a one. One that can stay as long as they want.

The temptation will always find you. It's one you want to resist because you know in order to get out of this without any attachments or cracks, you have to stay strong. You have to keep your distance. Distance is good. Distance allows your mind to fully comprehend that you can feel this with someone else. Someone who's permanent rather than temporary. Even though you wish it wasn't temporary.

So fight through the day. Instead of reaching for your phone late at night to send the text you're going to regret, close your eyes and think about something else. Think about how even though this is what you're craving right now that it, too, shall pass.

I've always been good at hiding those feelings. Those passionate feelings that sit in the pit of my stomach like a fire ready to explode but when someone ignites that fire there's no denying it. But instead of letting the fire consume me, I'm going to let it slowly burn out until it's no longer there. Until I find something permanent instead of temporary.

12

The Truth Behind Asking Someone, "What's Your Number?"

How many people have you slept with?

The question hung in the air between us. It was inevitable that he was going to ask but I was hoping it would have come later. It was question I often avoided, not because I was ashamed or had a number that was all that high, but it was just the purpose behind the question itself. He wasn't really asking how many people I had slept with.

What he was really asking was *how many people did you care about before me? How many people have you given a piece of yourself to? How many men am I competing with?* When I refused to answer the question and explained why it didn't matter was when everything ended. It was the things he said to me afterwards that made me start to question myself. He accused me of hooking up with people and using them without a care in the world. And when he uttered the phrase *you're such a guy* is when it felt like he had punched me in the gut.

As women, we have some high expectations to fill. We're supposed to be innocent virgins who magically know how to do everything and be everything in the bedroom. Our number of sexual partners needs to stay low and be completely accepting of our partner's high conquests. But men feel it, too. Men are supposed to have high numbers to seem like 'the man' amongst their friends. We do it to each other.

There is nothing wrong with having high numbers (as long as you're being safe!) or with having low numbers. The amount of sexual partners we have in our life time is not reflective of the soul beneath us.

Our ability to love one another is not based on what we have and haven't done in the bedroom. You can be promiscuous in a committed relationship without cheating. It's about finding what works for you and your significant other.

My best sexual encounter was my most recent. Why? It was amazing because I was able to be myself. There was no judgement. It was freeing. It had nothing to do with how many people either of us had been with and everything to do with the attraction and ability to just be who we are as humans. Sex forces vulnerability because in those moments it's really hard to be anything other than you.

So why is sex still this shameful thing? Why is it that what we do in our own bedroom is frowned upon when really if you look at any advertisement sex is the main sales technique?

It's because even though it's 'accepted' it's still not really accepted. We still have that old school thinking of sex being for procreation instead of recreation. And I fully support that but it's not this bad thing that we should feel bad about doing.

I'm not the person to believe that you need to be in love to have sex. I just have never been that person. Having said that, I have cared about every person I have been with. Maybe not in a 'romantic forever' way but definitely in a respect way.

My point is your body is your body. If you don't want to tell people how many people you've slept with then don't. If you want to sleep with someone then do it. Just don't feel like shit because you did. Every encounter you have with people, sexual or otherwise, should leave you feeling good about yourself and not awful. Ultimately at the end of the day if you can look yourself in the eye and know you made the right decision for you then that's all that matters.

13

This Is The Reality Behind Falling For Someone You Know Is Bad For You

It's the same dream. The same dream that used to be reality. There's something deep inside of him that feeds something so dark within me that it's the only thing that makes me feel sane. Maybe that was the draw to something I knew I should have stayed away from.

We got each other. From the second we met, we just got each other. Much to other people's chagrin. And even though we were completely wrong and unhealthy in every way, I lived for the late-night texts. I lived for those chance encounters. It was an addiction to see what was going to happen next. It was the complete rush of freedom that I felt when I was with him that made everything bad seem OK. Because there was *a lot* of bad.

I could see it in his soul, in his heart that there was something completely fucked up. It was fine, though, because it was the same fucked up that I knew all too well. You can have different backgrounds, come from different stories but still have the same insecurities and self-doubt that is completely mirrored.

The moments when it was just the two of us were the moments I liked. I didn't want anything else. I used him as sanctuary. I don't even know if I liked him much. Mostly because he reflected the parts of me I don't like. **So I gave him the acceptance and love I couldn't give myself.** It was easier that way.

I shouldn't have been surprised when he shut me out. I mean, I would have eventually done it, too. It was the nature of the game. As soon as something doesn't go the exact way I want it, then I leave it. It's much easier to leave it than to deal with it. But still it hurt when he decided for both of us that it wasn't working anymore. No conversation. No reasons. Just gone.

It made leaving easier. I was never in love with him or saw him as my future, but I still wanted to end things on my terms. Maybe that was my ego. He had gotten the leg up on me so it had pissed me off completely. And man, was I angry at him. Drunken texts from weeks previous had proven that to me. I had said things I didn't even know I could say. I had managed to express my feelings without backing down.

But was it the sex or the person I wanted? Was it the person who had told me the things I needed to hear versus the things I wanted to hear always that made me keep wanting to come back for more? No, that wasn't it. It was the fact that I wanted to be temporarily fixated on something other than myself. **I**

wanted to get lost in someone else's shit because my own is too much for me.

The problem with addiction is that if he ever popped back into my life I don't think I would be able to stop wanting him. Because his darkness is hauntingly beautiful. I feel the internal conflict of wanting to hate him but wanting to hold him. Wanting to punch him in the throat but wanting to kiss his temples. Wanting to let him go but wanting to know that he'll somehow always be around.

There is more to life than spending it with someone who can simultaneously make you feel alive while killing something deep within you. He drained me. He has made me question things about myself I didn't even know I felt awful about. Or maybe he just brought them to light. Brought the feelings I had managed to ignore for years. **Maybe his purpose was to make me deal with my insecurities.**

So he's given me a gift, really. He left before he could mess me up more and he showed me somethings I need to start fixing. And while I'll never thank him because I'm still so angry, so hurt from things that happened, I know that his purpose was to shine a light into my soul that only I could see.

And for that I could never hate him. Not even a little.

14

I Hate To Admit It, But I Can't Stop Thinking About What You To Do My Body

I'm so completely attached to you. You take me to the moon and back with just one touch. I just want to hear you say my name in a way that no one else can. Late at night. Breathy. Desperate. This connection has caused an effect on me I didn't know existed. It's a deep burn in the pit of my stomach causing me to crave you. *Only you.*

If we were in our right minds we'd know how terrible we are for each other. But I give in every single time because your intensity radiates off of you like a drug that I need. I want. I desire. The effect you have on me is palpable. You take me to a place of nirvana I've never been to before and that's why I know it's too late to walk away. **You feel too good for me to not give in to you.**

It's lips on lips. It's fingernails running down backs. It's two fucked up, likeminded individuals wanting temporary relief from their brains.

Because you and I are two people who get trapped inside

their own heads. But when we're together we get trapped inside each other. In a room full of people, I'll still be drawn to you first because no one sets my body on fire like you.

I don't want your last name but I want to hear you scream my first one. We both feel the same. We don't need to be each other's forever as long as we're each other's right now. No one would be able deny the chemistry that reacts as soon as our bodies touch. I know I sure can't. And it's not something I've felt before. We're both playing a part together right now. A part where love doesn't matter and all that matters is this.

It's a hunger. It's a thirst. It's instinctive. It's animalistic. It's one of those things you can't simply sum up in a sentence. They say you need love with sex for it to be amazing. But when I'm with you I know this isn't true. Because most of the time I down right hate you. Hate you for making me want you so badly I can't think about anything else.

It's *that* sex. The one you're thinking about right now. The one that pops into your mind when it's late at night and you're by yourself. It's the one that you use as a benchmark when your friends ask you who the best was. It's the one that still turns you on every time you think about it.

That's the one. That's this one. The one that envelops your brain when you're trying to think about anything else. The one that makes you want to quit your job and do nothing else with your days.

It's rough hands. Wandering fingers. Endless nights. And

when it ends and your body finally returns to earth, you wonder what the fuck just happened.

How someone could make you feel so alive and simultaneously make you question everything you knew before?

I don't know if I've heard anything hotter than when *oh baby* slips out of your mouth while your fingers are completely intertwined in my hair. It's not just the act itself but the ability to be free with you. Free to be myself in such a raw state is incredibly liberating. Honey, *you liberate me.*

So don't go. Don't slip out of my bedroom and kiss me on the forehead like every time before. Just stay. Stay and let's do this over and over again until we forget that anything outside of this exists. Let's get lost in each other. Because you take me to the highest highs and that's all I want. It's too late to run away from this. Let's just embrace it. Let's be each other's right now. We've got nothing to lose.

15

The Bitter And Beautiful Truth About Saying Something Is 'Just Sex'

Tell me what you want from me and I'll do anything.

The words were on replay in my brain as I stared into the eyes of darkness. Darkness I had been running from for the last while. I knew I should walk away but I couldn't as soon as I felt the sex that radiated from him from head to toe. And the way he did things to my body, it was almost revolutionary.

I know I should just walk away but I can't move. I can't move because his hold on me is so strong. All I want to do is get lost with him. Follow him down a dark path. A shadowy path where I found myself again. He had taken me to the depths of ecstasy that made me reconnect with my body in almost a spiritual way. He was bad but bad in all the right ways.

Deep down under all of the self-alluding wicked was an innocence. Something that made him worthy of the time that I wanted to spend with him. I didn't need anyone else to understand I just needed his hands on me. I just needed his mouth to bite at exposed skin. I just needed him to fulfill a role in my life that I had long forgotten I needed.

We were using each other. An escape from our realities that were so completely opposite. His reality was so much harsher than mine. His was filled with sorrow and pain while mine was filled with hope and disappointment.

But when we fit together, we weren't two people anymore. We were just this. We were just what we were doing in the moment. And while our lives had little in common, our bodies knew each other well. They just worked. Together.

One taste wasn't enough. One time had to be more than one time. And there was an unspoken promise that this, that what we were doing together, was just for us. Just for us and it was what it was and nothing more.

And even though I made that promise, the promise to not feel more than skin to skin contact, I let my heart feel it a bit, too. Forever and always I will have a soft spot for him even though everything inside my brain was screaming don't do it. Don't let him in. But it was too late. You don't feel that way naked and vulnerable without letting that person get under your skin.

He was completely under my skin. So deep under me that even when we were just breathing the same air space I couldn't concentrate. I wanted to run my hands through his hair and look into those eyes that made me squirm when they landed on me. I wanted him to grab my wrists and push me against the wall before his lips crashed against mine. I wanted him in every single bad way that I could think of.

He wasn't just a body to me. He couldn't ever mean so little. But I couldn't tell him that. Because even though our bodies matched completely, our emotions were entirely opposing. Our brains in their own ways made us remember that we're not good enough for each other. That we could never be good enough for each other. Our realities were just not going to ever be one in the same.

But if he ever wanted to live our fantasy again I'd be there in a heartbeat. Because even though it's wrong, I crave him and the way he felt next to me. And for the rest of my life I'll remember him for those intensely intimate moments; everything else is just details.

Part 4

The Heartbreak

16

What If I Told You I Missed You?

When I tell you I miss you don't confuse that with pining after you. In that moment, when we're speaking, I miss you. I don't sit around in sweatpants eating ice cream and wishing you were here and my life is unfulfilling without you… anymore. I don't think about you every day like I used to. You're not a memory that appears in my head constantly. I don't wonder where you are or what you're doing.

When your name pops up on my iPhone screen I'm momentarily sent back to when your name was a constant. When you weren't just a memory but my reality. When you weren't just letting me walk away without so much as hint of wanting to stop me. But yet you still talk to me. You even tell me that you miss me. That sucks.

It sucks to let someone go. To not fight for them. But then to tell them on a regular basis that you miss them. You didn't have to miss me. You *don't* have to miss me. You could have just had me. But that was your decision to make me feel like I wasn't worth it. **I wasn't worth your time. I wasn't worth arguing for.**

But I have major faults in this, too. I have so many of them. My ego is hard to deal with. I know that. We both knew that during and after every argument. My ego damages but my pride destroys. I didn't need you and I made damn sure you knew that. I made sure that when it comes to my life, I make the decisions and you, well, you get what's left over.

My ego. My pride. It's evident that I can't say it. I can't even let you think that maybe sometimes I do pine for you. That sometimes I do wear sweatpants, eat ice cream, and think about how amazing it would be if you were here. That I wish I could show you all of the new things in my world you're missing. That letting you go is something I struggle with daily. **That missing you has become so natural that it's just a feeling I bury deep within me.**

We both know that I'll never come back to you with my heart in my hands begging you to love me. That was pretty clear the last time we talked. I'm strong and I'm tough so you don't get to see the inside pieces of my heart anymore. The pieces that I've been trying to glue back together. The ones I assumed would magically fix themselves after time and miles between us.

But it doesn't work that way. Miles and time do work if you're willing to actively move on. If you're willing to put in the work to let the other person go. To be completely honest, I'm not ready yet. I'm not ready to pretend that seeing your name on my phone or in my inbox doesn't make my heart flutter because you want to talk to me. That you want to see how I am. That you still give a shit after all this time.

And really that's all my ego needs: **I need to know that I had an effect on your life the same way you had on mine.**

So is it ego or feelings that keep me holding onto you? Wanting to hear you tell me just one more time how great you think I am? Do I miss you, or do I miss the way you manage to always say the right things?

It's both. My feelings are real. They have to be. And as I have this internal struggle on paper it makes me realize why you let me go in the first place. My never-ending back and forth about who I am, what I want, and my feelings for you aren't fair to you.

So I don't pine for you; I crave you. I crave the feelings that were once so raw and so real to me. They seem like such a distant memory that they almost don't feel real anymore. You and I don't exist anymore. We never will again. So for now I'll just miss you. Because that's just where I am. And that's OK.

<u>17</u>

I Love Me More Than I Hate You

If you wanted me to hate you then you got your wish. I fucking *hate* you. Every single self-absorbed, douchebag piece. I could deal with your mountains of insecurities; hell, I could deal with the mean and cutting words, but lying is one thing I can never put up with. Especially people who can look another person in the eye and just lie.

I guess the worst part is I believed you. You fucked me and then you fucked me over. So congratulations, I hate you. I know this is what you wanted. Why anyone would ever want someone to hate them is beyond me but it's exactly what you wished for.

So I'll give it to you. Anger is a secondary emotion to hurt but I will never admit that you hurt me. My pride is too strong for that. You have managed to take pieces of me that I thought I had healed. I know no one can control your self-esteem or self-love but when someone is constantly telling you all of your shortcomings, tell me then how easy it is to not give in to their words and judgements.

And my friends warned me but I was too blinded by charm to see what the fuck you were. A serpent. A disgusting snake.

The worst kind of human. And you knew how to play me so well. You played into my need to give and knew that I would want to heal you. I should have been tough enough, smart enough to see that.

My fault was being naïve. Naïve and stupid. Stupid enough to believe that you had one good bone in your body. Your mind is vicious and your heart is completely fucked up. But your soul, your soul is made up of pure hatred. Because no one who knows what love is could ever treat any other human being the way you do.

And I know I'm not the only casualty of your cruelness. I'm not the only one you destroyed on your path to your self-ful-filling prophecy. The one where you convince yourself that you are a good person. You're not a good person.

Good people don't make others feel less than. They don't control them with horrible words or extort their insecurities. Good people love people in abundance regardless of their shortcomings. Regardless of if they measure up to some unimaginable standard you made up in your head. But loving other people would mean that you would have to love your-self.

And it's clear you don't. And, my dear, no matter how much I hate you, it's nowhere near how much you hate yourself. So for that, I pity you. I feel bad for you. Because love is so much better than hatred. Hating yourself is only going to leave you feeling empty and lonely. And that vacant feeling you have in your heart is going to stay. Don't ever think that because some else is warming the other side of your bed from time to time that you aren't completely and utterly alone.

Hate is a waste of an emotion, but I feel it pump through my veins when I see your name. But this is when I let that go. Because hating you for the rest of my life would only harm me. And I love me more than I hate you.

18

When You Need To Accept That Love Isn't Enough To Make It Work

There's a moment when you feel that it's over. It's just over. Somewhere down the line it went wrong and you just can't do it anymore. And it doesn't mean someone was bad. It's not how you expected it to go but it happened and you're crushed. Mostly because you were sure that this was it this time.

You go back to the first time you saw that person. She was swaying her hips drunkenly to the music at your friend's party. Or he was standing at the bar with his friends, laughing at something one of them had said. Either way, you remember that butterfly feeling and it makes you nostalgic for the better times. The times when nothing mattered except having to know their name. Wanting to touch their face. Craving to feel their lips on yours.

And by some divine miracle you ended up meeting. Whether you worked up the courage to eventually tap them on the shoulder or you bumped into each other later in the night, you met. And it was exactly what you thought it was going to be. It was an instant feeling of pure joy that made you feel incredibly cheesy thinking that these were the moments in life that you live for. It was the buzzing that you felt throughout your entire body after the first kiss that sealed everything.

Then you dive in head first. There were no games. No pretending that you didn't like each other. In your friend's minds, you were both borderline obsessed with each other. God, who doesn't like that? Just feeling the extreme highs that come with getting into a relationship with another person who feels the exact same way you do.

We hear about the relationships that end because of cheating or some other major issue but we rarely hear of the ones that just fizzle out. That there isn't anyone to blame, it's just over. **And those are the saddest to me. The ones where both partners just can't figure out why it's not working anymore. Why they don't feel the same way that they did before.** You both know, too. That there's something just a little off. That things are just a little too forced lately. That even seeing them naked doesn't get you as stoked as it used to. And it used to get you extremely stoked. And you feel bad. Because it has nothing to do with them or their body and everything to do with where you're at. And where they're at. Because you both know you're going through the motions instead of feeling.

No matter how much you love the person, sometimes it just doesn't work. And it's nothing they did. Nothing you said. Nothing at all that really contributed to the break. You just have your path and they have theirs. And unfortunately, the paths just don't intertwine. They don't magically end up together.

It still hurts. When things just don't work out. It hurts like hell because there really is no real reason other than the fact that you just don't fit together.

So you both pick up the pieces of your hearts and try to repair them in the ways that you know how to. Eventually you go to another party or bar and look up to see someone new who gives you that same butterfly feeling you had before. And that excitement reminds you why love is so great. No matter what happened before, in that moment you remember why you let yourself fall in love in the first place.

And that feeling alone is worth it. It just is.

19

Read This If You're Constantly Hung Up On The Past And Need To Remember Why You Left It Behind

There are some people in this world that continue to affect you even long after they're gone. It's that gravitational pull that messes with you and makes you wonder what exactly the universe is trying to tell you by bringing these people in and out of your life.

Maybe that's why on a random Thursday night I was in the same dimly-lit bar I frequented once every few months. His text just says "drinks?" and I know exactly when and where. I know because we've been doing this for years now.

It's funny how we know we need to let go of someone but we continue to allow ourselves to get trapped in the same scenarios. That's because every time that person contacts you, whether it be a text, email, or phone call, it's like someone pushed the reset button. And then it's like all the feelings you had pushed aside are ready to just explode again. Unless you're strong enough to just not. To not indulge in the temptation of seeing that person and hear what they have to say. I wasn't strong enough to leave this piece behind yet.

Maybe that's why I was spending my Thursday night with someone I see quarterly, if that. He sits in the same place every time. Orders the same drink for me and for him every time. And I look down at his silver ring on his left hand thinking about how it wasn't there when we first met. We have the same heart-to-heart about what exactly is bothering him this time except I already know. Then we take a trip down memory lane when we used to listen to music in the back of his truck bed and make out under the stars.

Maybe that's what draws us back to a person.

Maybe it's the memories of the good times back when things were simpler and you lived for just each other. Or maybe it's just simply that we hold tight to the things we don't want to let go of just yet. Five years later, I should have let go of him the second he walked away. Not because he was bad but because we no longer served each other. We served each other's egos.

Eventually the conversation will circle around to how we should have probably ended up together. We'll end up staring at each other silently wondering what would have been different if we had just made things work. If we just weren't too young. If we weren't just too dumb. If I was a little tamer and he was a little wilder. If we figured out that maybe, just maybe, this was worth fighting for.

But like all good what ifs, we come back to the real world

and see we're exactly where we're supposed to be. We all go through periods of our lives where we always think the grass would be greener if we had just made a different decision. But if you look at those choices and where they've led you, most of the time you wouldn't take anything back. You'd continue with your path because ultimately this is where you want to be and what works for you.

Our lives are not made up of right or wrong choices. It's made from the best possible choice or the choice that felt right in the moment. We could spend years analyze every conversation, every interaction, every painful moment and try to figure out how everything would have gone if we had just done something a little different.

Looking back at those brown eyes that pull me in every time, that Thursday will be the last time we see each other. It was time to not only grow up but also stop using each other as a crutch. We made the decisions we made back then and we continue to make the ones that led us down different paths in the first place. So let go of the things that no longer serve you.

Because when the past comes calling, it really has nothing new to say.

20

I Need You To Choose Me Forever This Time Or Finally Let Me Go

I remember what it felt like when you left. I remember my best friend trying to pick up the pieces that were scattered around me. I remember feeling like the wind had been knocked completely out of my chest and it was a struggle to even remember to breathe. I remember the exact moment you left, the reason, and why you made the choice you did.

I remember all of that. So when you send me an out of the blue *how are you?* text, it takes me right back to that moment. The moment I had to learn how to start being OK without you. I had managed to gather up the bits of my life that I had intertwined in you and retaught myself how to go to bed at night alone. So out-of-the-blue texts to see how I'm doing, to ask if I'm OK, to wonder where I am, are punishing. They're disruptive. They're exactly the opposite of what you should do.

When you apologize for what happened it doesn't make anything better. It makes me remember why you feel the need to apologize in the first place. It reminds me that I didn't feel enough then and in the months that have passed, I haven't really found former self yet still. I don't benefit from your selfish apologies. All you really want is for me to give you the relief of saying *It's OK* or *Don't worry about it* but this time I won't give that to you. Because the truth is, you hurt me.

What really bothers me is that I get caught up in your conversation every time. Every single time. I want it to go on for days. I don't want you to stop talking to me. I don't want to go back to not reading your messages on my phone, even if it is just a painful reminder of the past. I miss the past when it was you and me. I want the times back when I laughed so hard that my cheeks hurt. I want the feeling of wanting to go to sleep with you and wake up in that very same bed. I want the deeply rooted fear of being abandoned again to be gone. **I want it to be us again.**

So sure, I'll go out and catch the eye of someone new. And sometimes I'll ask him to fill the space that you left. But more often than not, it's just me. It's just me thinking about what we had and what we lost. And I understand your reasons. I understand why we couldn't be an 'us' anymore. I get it all. What I don't get is how as soon as I'm starting to let you go, you manage to pop back up. How you manage to completely derail my life all over again.

My heart can't take the push and pull. It can't take the touch and go. It certainly can't stand the back and forth. It wants you to either go or stay but no in between. No indecision.

Either choose *us* or don't choose me at all.

Because I'll no longer answer the *U up?* or the *How are you?*

texts. Why? It's not fair to either of us to continue to keep each other as a life line. You were my life support. But now I've found a way to breathe without you and that's a trend I'd like to continue.

21

How To Heal (Really Heal) From Heartbreak

It feels different now.

You're still hurt. I mean, of course you are. It was the biggest pain of your life and that just doesn't heal over night. But you've been going through hell to get over them and now it's starting to hurt a little less. Then you start to breathe again, a little easier. Like the way you did before that knife was shoved through your windpipe. It'll never be exactly the way it was before but it will start to feel better.

Sometimes you'll give into the temptation of drinking your feelings away. You'll find comfort in things you know you shouldn't but you do anyway. We all have tricks and ways to ensure that our heart heals as painlessly as possible.

Because getting your heart broken fucking sucks.

It's hard to believe that there are things out there that feel worse than this. But this excruciating part of heartbreak will eventually end. It will get easier. And you'll be stronger.

And man, have you gone through some shit to feel even just a little better. Even if you knew that your relationship was on borrowed time, in the end it doesn't matter. It hurts sometimes before it even ends. Because even though we know something's over, there's a difference between jumping and being pushed. We all want to do things on our terms. We're all selfish that way.

But little by little, piece by piece, day by day, you get back to you. The you that you remember being before this person. The person who was radiating positivity and love. Not this sad, heartbroken person you've been. The one who feels like a burden to their friends because all you can talk about is the person who left you or who you left.

What can you do other than to feel the feelings? Acknowledge that they exist. Learn from them. Talk about them until you're sick of saying the words and your friends are sick of hearing them. You need to let yourself go around and around until you understand what you're feeling and what exactly the issue is. Because even though we want to blame the other person for hurting us, there's usually two sides to every breakup. Not always. But usually.

You could've lied. You could've told people it was all great when it was not. You could've tried to go on living without ever thinking about that person again. You could've said you don't think about them late at night. You could've pretended you don't text them every now and then to see how they're doing. You could've done all of those things and denied the fact that losing the person you thought was your forever wasn't as hard as it has been.

But you didn't. You embraced the hurt. You have done your

healing. And now it doesn't hurt like it used to. It still hurts. There are still times you wonder what happened. But it doesn't feel like it did. You still slip back into old habits from time to time. Sometimes you even cry about it. But you know that whatever happened, happened because it wasn't right. For either of you.

You've made it through the hellish part. Now all you have to do is keep going and know that love, the right kind of love, will make it to you when you least expect it.

Part 5

The Love

22

Everything About You Scares Me, Which Is Why I Want To Love You

You have caught me so off guard. You're everything I know I don't need right now but want so bad. There's a second when you're in my space that I feel like I'm suffocating because your intensity, your beauty, and your smarts knock me backwards. It makes me wonder and believe that all the people I've met before were guiding me to this moment. The moment where when we speak to each other I feel like I'm home. **Because home isn't necessarily a place, but a feeling.**

Right now we're both not in a place to love each other. To give each other the support we need in order to be good enough to work. Maybe it's because we're both two very free spirits who don't even know the direction we should go. All I know is that our directions should be the same. Because with you I manage to be able to be more me. Slowly but surely there will be points where I question you because you're not something I'm used to. *Stability.* **Even if everything else around us and within our own universes is complete and utter chaos, you stand tall and true as steadiness.**

It's a feeling. I just feel it in my gut. I said *Oh shit!* the minute

I saw you because deep down inside I felt that you were going to be something. And you are something. What? I'm not so sure yet. But I want to be sure. I want to be sure that you're not going to be gone tomorrow. And every indication points to you not disappearing.

When you meet people sometimes they just ignite something in your bones. You feel it like an electric shock sent straight through your entire body. And you need to see them again. **You're almost too afraid to see them again. Because they're captivating and make your heart want to explode out of your chest.** You see the true beauty in their expressions and mannerisms. Those weird mannerisms that makes someone them. That's how I feel about you.

And I'm excited. It's the kind of excited I've been before but haven't felt in a while. You're not a chore. Not someone who's emotionally draining. You're just you, and honey, just you is perfectly all right with me. When you look at me I feel like we have a secret understanding, a private joke, that no one else is privy to.

But then the fear sets in. The belief that maybe, just maybe I'm not enough. I'm scared that I won't be able to offer you enough. I'm afraid that I'm just not enough. I mean we've both seen and felt what happens when it doesn't work out. We both know pain even if we've felt it in extremely different ways. Pain is pain and we both have been the victims of this cruel mistress but we both survived. And we're here.

I can tell you that the fear is almost enough to make me walk away. It's almost enough to make me not want to dive back into something that leaves me vulnerable and at the mercy of someone else. But letting the potential for love slip away is worse than going through the hurt again. **In this instance, there is nothing to lose and everything to gain, because sweetheart, you'd definitely be worth my wounded ego and hurt pride if for even just a millisecond I get to hold you.**

So I'm going to weather this storm. I'm going to go full force into it and hope that somehow I make it out with little to no damage. That somehow if there's a hurricane coming for me that you're there to guide me through it.

There's just something in the way you say my name that makes me realize that I have nothing to lose and you to gain. So let's go on this adventure together and see where it takes us, shall we?

23

I Love You Enough To Let You Go

With you I'm more me. That's not an easy feat. This is an accomplishment that you should really take to heart. Being fully myself with someone is not something I do. I actually very rarely do it. The real me is quiet, introspective, and shy. You bring that out of me. You make me feel safe.

So how do you thank someone who's allowed you to be real? How do you thank someone who makes you feel like you're worth something? The answer is you don't.

You can't ever thank them enough, and even if you do, they're not going to think you need to. They won't understand their affect and how much they've changed your inner workings. They won't understand that they're important, so fucking important that ultimately they scare you.

There's so much weight put on the word love, like it's the be-all and end-all but I love people on a regular basis without the expectation that they're going to be my one. There are soul mates we have who are here just for a while. To teach us lessons we need to learn in order to get to where we're going.

I think I freak people out when I use the word love because I use it often. Sometimes I feel like I need to say all the words but I'm learning that the best thing I can do for the people I love is just let them be. Sometimes walking away is the right option even though it feels like it's not. We always think it's weak to walk away without telling someone our true feelings, but in some cases, it's the only option.

In order to keep the person you love from falling apart sometimes you have to let them go. I love hard. I love intensely. I love being able to give love. But my heart is hurting. It's hurting because even though I want to be vulnerable I can't. I can't give someone the words they need or the space they deserve because of my own selfish need to love. I cause pain on a daily basis with my love. But we all do. In some ways love is selfish. It fills our heart with meaning. It gives us a reason to get out of bed.

I want to tell you everything before I go but I know I can't. The girl who can write about anything can't even be real with her feelings and say the words. Maybe that's because the words aren't right. Everything in my head is jumbled. It's coming out confusing. My feelings are bubbling over and I just want nothing more than for you to hug me. Because I feel safe when you hug me.

I knew what I was getting myself into. I knew that I had to be the one to be strong. I knew ultimately this was going to happen. It's hard when you have a pattern to not see it when it's repeating. But this isn't the same. I've never allowed someone to see the parts of me that you have. You came at a time in my life when I needed you most and for that I definitely thank you.

So it comes down to this; I love you enough to walk away. Do I think it's the kind of love that stops my entire world? No. But you are not someone that's easy for me to let go of. You're so much more than what you give yourself credit for and it kills me to know you don't see it. All I can do now is give you the space and hope that ultimately our paths cross again.

24

What If I Told You I Love You?

What if I told you everything I've been hiding so deep inside? If I just looked you in the eyes and told you every single insecurity that plagues me daily. Or how about how I just don't feel good enough for you. Because I don't. I don't feel like I've been the person worthy of loving you. But I'm so lucky that I get to.

What if I told you every single thing I've done wrong in my life? If I sat you down and outlined every single mistake I've ever made. Would you leave? Would you love me more? Would you laugh it off? Because me telling you everything would make you the most important person to me. Are you ready for that?

What if I told you I've never loved someone as much as you? Would it freak you out? Would it make you look for the door? Because I've never loved someone this much. I've never had this much to lose. I've never thought about loving someone as deeply and intensely as I love you. I just never thought this love would ever come to someone like me. And now that you're here I don't want you to go anywhere.

What if I told you that all the stupid things I've done that

I've blamed on other people? Would you think less of me? Would you question my character? Would it make you rethink everything that you've felt about me this far? Or would you take my hand and tell me that it's OK. That we're OK. That this right now feels better than anything you've ever felt, too.

What if I told you that sometimes I'm crazy? And I don't mean crazy fun. I mean the kind of crazy that will be too much for you sometime. The kind that will in turn make you feel crazy yourself. I'll tell you right now you're not doing anything wrong. I just can't help myself in indulging in a little crazy every now and then. But it'll keep you on your toes.

What if I told you that I have a gypsy soul? That staying in one place gives me itchy feet? That I want to see what the world has to offer? Would you think that I was leaving because of you? Because it's not. I want you to come, too. I want you to be my partner in crime. I want you to see the world with me. I want you to be my travel companion.

What if I told you that I've been hurt before and this scares me? Scares me so much that sometimes I think you're fake. That you aren't someone who exists in this world. That you're going to disappear just like the exes before you. That I want so badly to pretend that we're good. That this is good. But I just can't keep the negativity out of my head sometimes.

What if I told you that I've hurt someone really bad before? Would you be afraid of me? I could tell you that it was because it just fizzled out but really it was because I didn't feel it. I just didn't feel it anymore. You know that feeling the one that you just feel deep down in your bones? That's this. It wasn't that.

What if I told you I love you?

Would you say it back? Would it be too soon? Would our friends call us crazy? The answer is a resounding yes. To everything. Because you always do say it back. Because I knew I loved you when we met. Because our friends call us crazy on a regular basis. We're crazy because we love each other more deeply than either of us has felt.

There are a lot of what ifs, but our relationship isn't one of them. It's not a *What if we decided not to do this anymore?* because that's not an option. For either of us. And we prove that to each other daily. So I'll tell you every stupid thing I've done. I'll tell you every single lie I've ever told. I'll tell you anything you want to know because I love you.

That's the only thing I do know for sure.

25

9 Things I Can't Wait To Tell My Future Husband

Dear Future Husband,

No this isn't the start of a Meghan Trainor song, although that would be pretty cool. I don't think we've met yet but I'm really hoping we do soon. I have a few things I want to tell you because, let's be honest, we both know I'm not the easiest to crack open sometimes.

Number 1: I'm really sorry for being stubborn.

My family and friends will tell you that I'm stubborn and I'll deny it, but hell, they're right. I'm going to fight you tooth and nail to prove that I'm right, most of the time I am. I promise you though that I will always apologize when I'm wrong;, which will hopefully be close to never.

Number 2: My first love left a really deep scar.

It's true. Like most people in this world, my first love did a real number on me. He made me doubt my worth and who I was as a person. But I think you probably already know that. Thanks for always being patient with me when I get irrationally mad when we both know you did nothing wrong. You're awesome.

Number 3: You are the best I've ever had.

This is a big thing. Maybe there are better lovers out there but for me you will always be the best because I chose you and you chose me to spend the rest of our lives together. Because of this fact alone you are the best in every way.

Number 4: I tell my best girl friend everything that happens between us.

I mean, you've met her and I'm sure you know we talk about you. She knows every weird thing that we've laughed about and every embarrassing moment you've had, past and present. I tell her this because I am so incredibly in love and proud of you that I'm telling her these things so she can also love you almost as much as I do.

Number 5: You're my best friend.

There's no question to this. While I'll have good girl and guy friends, and call some of them my best friends, when it comes to my ultimate best friend, that's you. You know every deep, dark secret I've kept close to my heart so how could you not be my best friend? You deserve that title, especially if you've put up with me when I'm hangry.

Number 6: You're freaking hot.

I promise I'll tell you how hot you are on a regular basis. I'll make sure you never forget how wanted you are and how even on the roughest of days you are my shining light. Even if you're the reason I'm mad.

Number 7: You're stuck with me.

We said those vows, mister, which means I'm not going anywhere. You don't get a piece of me, you get the whole darn thing, and that means I'm not backing down when things get tough. We will work through it because I love you.

Number 8: Thank you for being a part of my family and letting me be a part of yours.

Sure, mine is little crazy but they love you almost as much as I do. Does it get annoying that I call my mom every night? Maybe. Is it also a little excessive that I tell her when you're being a jerk? Definitely. But know that she never fully believes you're the issue and mostly ends up taking your side.

Number 9: I'm going to love the crap out of you.

I don't care what you've done, where you've been, or who you've hurt. If you are willing to be there for me, care for me, and love me then I'm going to do the same in return. So often we get caught up in who we were that we lose sight of what we have to offer. Babe, you've got everything I need so I will love the crap out of you forever.

However long you take to get to me know this: I am getting ready to love you to the best of my ability. I am working on taking care of myself so that when you show up we can start our lives together as two wholes rather than broken pieces we try to glue together.

Thank you for getting to know the real me and for loving every single thing I thought would hinder me from ever falling in love. You have shown me what true love is and for that I will forever be in your debt.

All my love always,

Your Future Wife.

26

When Someone Feels Like Home You'll Never Forget Them

I don't care where our paths are leading. I don't care that right now yours is different than mine. I don't care that you're millions of miles away. I don't care as long as somewhere down the line we meet back up.

Because baby, when that happens, it's going to be pure and utter magic.

I know you have to go. I know you have to find yourself. I know that there are so many things in this world we have to experience apart in order for us to work together. The nights are going to feel endless without you. The days are going to drag. But I know we're doing the right thing. I'm not going to stop you from going because I love you too much to do that.

But I'm going to miss you. Every single second you're gone. I'm going to miss the way you smell. The way you laugh. Your dimples. Your eyes. Everything. And even though you're not in my arms, you will always be in my heart. That's where you belong, anyway. There are going to be days when it's unbearable to know that you're not just a phone call away anymore.

There are going to be times when I'm going to be so close to cracking and will want to ask you to come back.

But I won't. I won't not for a lack of love but because I know if I did call, you'd come running. And I can't do that to you yet.

And if you ever called me, if you ever needed to hear my voice, to hear me tell you how amazing you are, I will always answer. If you ever felt like giving up or like the world was caving in, I would come find you. I would find you to tell you how incredibly strong you are. To give you the motivation you need to keep going. I will forever and always be your strength during your times of weakness.

So go.

Get out of here and don't look back. Because if you do look back or hesitate for a second, I'm going to break. I'm going to lose my nerve that's telling me to let you go. I'm going to forget everything about how it's right for us to separate for a bit and tell you to never leave. I'm going to put my needs above yours and I'm going to be incredibly selfish.

As bad as I want to ask you to stay, I know what you're meant to do. You're meant for more than this place. You're meant to see the world and discover things that not many people have the opportunity to. There's no way that I can go with you because in some ways that will hold you back. So chase those feelings that are telling you go and hold on to them in your darkest times.

Because they will get you through the lonely.

If I'm holding you back at all, know that I'll be all right. I'll be all right because you have given me the inspiration to find myself.

So maybe it's naïve to think that this will work out. That magically we will end up together. That we won't meet other people along the way. That we won't be led astray from this love between us. And maybe we will. But I trust in the feelings I get around you. That kinda love isn't just something you throw away.

Because when someone feels like home, you don't forget them.

The Rest

So what's the rest? Where do we go from here? What do we do with the love we've found or the love we've lost? Is it going to work out? Will this time your love work out? Or will you find the person you've always been looking for tomorrow?

My answer is this: I have no fucking idea.

Not a fucking clue. And that's because love is such a guessing game. One day we can be completely and utterly in love with someone we're pretty sure we're going to spend the rest of our lives with and then the next be completely lost. The human heart is something that I have yet to understand but cannot stop being fascinated with.

Love will come and love will go, but I do know this: every single time you let yourself be vulnerable to love, you win. You completely win because experiencing love of any kind—be it friendship, family, or romantic—is something that cannot be replicated in any other fashion.

There are people who would disagree with me. They'd choose money over passion, work over family, power over, well…anything else. To those people I say, *fair*. Love comes in many different forms for people. And the way we all experience and accept love is unique.

Whatever love you want or desire, know that it's worth it. But you have to work for it. It's a second full-time job finding love or being in a relationship. It's something people struggle to hold on to all the time because we get distracted by additional things like our jobs or other commitments. We forget that love isn't something that is just there whenever we need it. It's something we take on, and when we do, we have to give it everything or there's a chance we can lose it.

Don't lose it. Promise me that if you get it, you won't let it go easily. Fight for it. Remind the person you love daily that you would do anything for them. Make them feel wanted. Make them know that everything in your world that's worth having is because of them. And that should be true. Because they are your unwavering support. They're there to pick you up when you've fallen down. They just love you, as you are, and wouldn't change a thing about you.

And if you're not in love, well, my dear, the best is yet to come for you. When you give up on love and give up on its existence, you lose. There are going to be hard times. You're going to think about giving up. You'll be on your knees in your darkest hour just wishing, praying that someone would just love you. Just remember that someone does love you. Whether you're in a relationship or not, you are completely loved by someone. Hang on to that in those moments when you look in the mirror telling yourself that you're not worth loving.

As for me, well, I'm not sure about that, either. I have been so lucky to have loved so many people so far in my short 25 years on this planet. I have been hurt. I have been loved. I have lost. But I have picked myself up, and I work on getting better at seeing these endings a road block instead of the entire destruction of my path.

So continue to believe in love. Continue your path. Find out who you are in the process. Decide on what you'll accept and what you won't. Be you. No matter what. If you keep that in mind, there's no way you can ever lose.

About the Author

Alex is a Canadian transplant living in the UK. She falls in love fast and hard which makes her the ultimate expert on what not to do. She's the master of asking too many questions when it comes to people's romantic lives but that fuels her research on the ever-changing topic of love.

Thought Catalog, it's a website.
www.thoughtcatalog.com

Social
facebook.com/thoughtcatalog
twitter.com/thoughtcatalog
tumblr.com/thoughtcatalog
instagram.com/thoughtcatalog

Corporate
www.thought.is

www.ingramcontent.com/pod-product-compliance
Lightning Source LLC
Chambersburg PA
CBHW032113280326
41933CB00009B/825